TAKE THE NEXT STEP - VIRAL THREADS

ASHOK M

TABLE OF CONTENTS

HOW TO SET UP YOUR WINNING PROFILE

STEPS TO SET UP A WINNING PROFILE ON INSTAGRAM THREADS

1. CHOOSE A GOOD PROFILE PICTURE: USE IT AS AN IMPRESSION SINCE, ACCORDING TO MOST AUTHORITIES, THAT'S ONE OF THE KEY IMPRESSIONS PEOPLE WILL HAVE. USE A LARGE, CLEAR, HIGH-QUALITY IMAGE OF A BRAND, LOGO, OR ANYTHING SPECIFIC TO YOUR NICHE, SUCH AS HERBAL PRODUCTS, WELLNESS, OR WHATEVER ELSE THAT MIGHT DEFINE YOUR BRAND AND WHAT YOU REPRESENT. IT NEEDS TO BE CLEAR, PROFESSIONAL-LOOKING AND INTERESTING AT SMALL SIZES.

2. WRITE A COMPELLING BIO PURPOSE: YOUR BIO NEEDS TO SHOUT OUT WHO YOU ARE, TO WHOM, AND WHAT THEY WOULD EXPECT FROM YOU.

DETAILS: KEEP YOUR BIO SUCCINCT YET BENEFIT-DRIVEN. HIGHLIGHT YOUR NICHE AND AREA OF SPECIALTY, AND WHAT THE FOLLOWER WILL GAIN FROM YOU—

FOR EXAMPLE: "HERBAL ENTHUSIAST | SHARING AYURVEDIC WISDOM & NATURAL REMEDIES FOR HOLISTIC WELLNESS.". INCORPORATE THE RELEVANT KEYWORDS TO MAKE YOUR PROFILE DISCOVERED.

3. INSTALLATION OF A PRE-FILLED CALL-TO-ACTION PURPOSE: NUDGE THE VISITORS TO THE NEXT STEP.

DETAILS: INSTALL A BUTTON ON YOUR WEBSITE, BLOG, OR LEAD MAGNET WITH A STRONG CALL-TO-ACTION;

FOR EXAMPLE, DOWNLOAD YOUR FREE HERBAL GUIDE OR SHOP OUR BEST-SELLING AYURVEDIC PRODUCTS. UPDATE YOUR CALL-TO ACTION ACCORDING TO THE RUNNING PROMOTIONS OR LATEST MATERIAL EVERY NOW AND THEN.

4. FOCUS WISELY USE PURPOSE: ORGANIZE AND MAKE REALLY USEFUL CONTENT EASILY ACCESSIBLE.

DETAILS: THIS CAN BE DONE IN CREATING HIGHLIGHT REELS TO GROUP VALUABLE CONTENT INTO CATEGORIES, SUCH AS "TIPS," "RECIPES," "TESTIMONIALS," AND "FAQS." THIS MAKES YOUR PROFILE FEEL PRETTY ORGANIZED AND HELPS A NEWLY GAINED FOLLOWER REALIZE THERE'S PLENTY MORE TO EXPLORE.

5. CONSISTENT BRANDING PURPOSES CREATE A LOOK AND FEEL FOR YOUR BRAND.

DETAILS: CHOOSE A COLOR SCHEME AND FONT STYLE THAT WORKS WITH YOUR BRAND. KEEP YOUR THREADS POSTS TO BE AESTHETICALLY PLEASING AND CONSISTENT SO YOUR PROFILE BECOMES INSTANTLY RECOGNIZABLE. USE TEMPLATES FOR THE COMMON CONTENT TYPES, SUCH AS QUOTES OR TIPS.

6. TOP CONTENT STUCK TO YOUR PROFILE:

GOAL: SHOWCASE YOUR BEST THREADS.

DESCRIPTION: STICK TOP-PERFORMING OR MOST RELEVANT CONTENT ON TOP OF YOUR PROFILE, SO NEW VISITORS WILL VIEW YOUR TOP POSTS FIRST. THESE CAN BE INTROS, VIRAL POSTS, OR IMPORTANT ANNOUNCEMENTS.

7. KEYWORDS FOR DISCOVERABILITY PURPOSES:

HELP PEOPLE DISCOVER YOUR PROFILE BETTER.

DETAILS: USE KEYWORD-RELATED PHRASES IN THE NAME AND BIO ALSO SO THAT IF FOR

EXAMPLE: IF YOU ARE AN EXPERT IN AYURVEDA, YOU CAN WRITE "AYURVEDA EXPERT" OR SIMPLY "NATURAL HEALTH TIPS." THIS WILL INCREASE YOUR VISIBILITY WHEN A PERSON USES THE SEARCH OPTION.

8. WELCOME FIRST THREAD PURPOSE: WELCOME WITH A BANG.

FACTS: YOUR VERY FIRST POST WOULD BE PINNED AND AN INTRODUCTION TO YOU OR YOUR BRAND. SHARE YOUR STORY, YOUR MISSION, AND WHAT VALUE ONE CAN LOOK FORWARD TO. ADD A PERSONAL TOUCH IN BUILDING AN INSTANT CONNECTION.

9. INTERESTING STUFF PURPOSE: MAKE PEOPLE FEEL LIKE THEY'RE PART OF A COMMUNITY AND HAVE AN OPPORTUNITY TO INTERACT.

DETAILS: ASK QUESTIONS, SURVEY FOLLOWERS, AND PROMPT YOUR FOLLOWERS TO DO SOMETHING THROUGH YOUR POSTS. ENGAGE WITH COMMENTS AND INTERACT WITH FOLLOWERS TO DEVELOP RELATIONSHIPS.

10. MORE OFTEN: WELL, GOOD STUFF
PURPOSE: KEEP THE PROFILE UP,
INTERESTING, AND ACTIVE.

DETAILS: CONTINUOUSLY PROVIDE QUALITY
ITEMS THAT ARE USEFUL, INSPIRING,
INTERESTING, BEHIND-THE-SCENES, AND
USER-GENERATED CONTENT. REGULARITY
MAKES FOLLOWERS BELIEVE THAT THE
PROFILE IS WORTH FOLLOWING AND
SOMETIMES EVEN WORTH CHECKING BACK
IN ON.

FOLLOW THESE STEPS, AND YOU WILL HAVE
A PREPARED INSTAGRAM THREADS PROFILE
READY TO PERFORM WELL ON ENGAGEMENT
GROWTH AND CONVERSION.

HOW TO WRITE VIRAL SHORT-FORM THREADS

CREATING VIRAL SHORT-FORM THREADS: ENGAGE AND CONVERT

STEP 1: HOOK THE ATTENTION PURPOSE: GRAB THE READER'S ATTENTION IMMEDIATELY.

DETAILS: USE A BOLD STATEMENT, THOUGHT-PROVOKING QUESTION, OR SURPRISING FACT THAT GENERATES AN APPEAL BASED ON PAIN POINTS OR DESIRES IN YOUR AUDIENCE.

FOR EXAMPLE: "DID YOU KNOW THAT 70% OF THE PEOPLE ARE LOSING OUT ON NATURE'S REMEDIES THAT CAN TRANSFORM THEIR HEALTH?" THAT WILL MAKE THEM READ FURTHER.

STEP 2: BREAK UP THE CONTENT INTO BITES THAT ARE MORE PALATABLE

PURPOSE: KEEP YOUR READER ENGAGED.

DETAILS: USE SHORT, PUNCHY SENTENCES AND CLEAR PARAGRAPHS TO FORMAT YOUR THREAD. USE NUMBERED LISTS OR BULLET POINTS TO KEEP THE EMPHASIS OR MESSAGE SIMPLE AND READABLE.

STEP 3. DELIVER VALUE LIKE INSIGHTS OR TIPS

GOAL: TRUST AND AUTHORITY BUILDING,

CONTENT: SHARE VALUABLE TIPS, INTERESTING PERSPECTIVES, OR PERSUASIVE DATA RELATED TO YOUR NICHE. IF YOU TALK ABOUT HERBAL OR AYURVEDIC GOODS, SHARE BRIEF INSIGHTFUL TIPS ON WHAT THEY ARE GOOD FOR OR HOW UNIQUE USAGE IS POSSIBLE WITH THAT PRODUCT.

STEP 4. ADDING VISUALS

PURPOSE: TO BE ENGAGING.

DETAILS: ACCOMPANY THIS ARTICLE WITH IMAGES, INFOGRAPHICS, OR EMOJIS TO BREAK UP A BLOCK OF TEXT AND PROVIDE VISUAL APPEAL. THE RESPONSE WILL BE OF MORE INTEREST AND MEMORABILITY.

STEP 5. USE REAL VOICE

PURPOSE: TIES WITH PERSONALITY.

DETAILS: TALK IN YOUR BRAND VOICE, WHICH TRANSLATES INTO THE TONE THAT BRINGS OUT YOUR PERSONALITY. CREATE A STORY OR PERSONAL EXPERIENCES TO RESONATE WITH THE READER.

STEP 6. SOFT CTA MID-THREAD

PURPOSE: DRIVE READER ACTION WITHOUT BEING OVERTLY PROMOTIONAL IN YOUR MESSAGING.

DETAILS: ADD A SOFT NUDGE LIKE "WANT MORE TIPS LIKE THESE? FOLLOW ME FOR DAILY INSIGHTS!" AND CONTINUE ENGAGING THOSE READING.

STEP 7. END WITH A STRONG CTA

PURPOSE: BRING THE READER TOWARD SOME END GOAL ON YOUR PART.

MORE INFORMATION: END THE CONVERSATION WITH A STRONG AND COMPELLING CTA SUCH AS "READY TO TAKE THE CHANGE OF YOUR WELLNESS? CHECK OUT OUR [LINK/PRODUCT/SERVICE] NOW!" HIGHLIGHT THE VALUE THEY GET OUT OF THIS.

STEP 8: OPTIMIZE FOR VIRALITY

PURPOSE: DRIVE SHARES AND ENGAGEMENT

DETAILS: CREATE CONTENT THAT'S LIKELY TO PICK INTEREST OR CREATE A DEBATE. ASK QUESTIONS AT THE BOTTOM OF YOUR THREAD, SUCH AS "WHICH OF THESE TIPS SURPRISED YOU THE MOST? DISCUSS IN THE COMMENTS!" REACH OUT EARLY TO COMMENTERS TO GET THE DISCUSSION STARTED.

STEP 9. ANALYZE AND ITERATE

GOAL: IMPROVE YOUR STRATEGY FOR BETTER OUTCOMES.

INFORMATION: TRACK ENGAGEMENT METRICS: LIKES, SHARES, COMMENTS. DETERMINE WHICH THREADS WORK THE BEST, AND ADAPT YOUR APPROACH BASED ON WHAT IS MOST RESONATING WITH YOUR AUDIENCE.

STEP 10. BONUS TIP: FOLLOW-UP THREADS

GOAL: SUSTAIN THE STREAK. INFORMATION: HAVE A FOLLOWUP WITH MORE RELATED CONTENT OR "PART 2" TO CONTINUE ENGAGING YOUR AUDIENCE WITH THE THOUGHT OF SOMETHING ABOUT TO HAPPEN.

THESE ARE SOME STRATEGIES THAT CAN ENSURE YOUR SHORT-FORM THREADS CAPTURE THE ATTENTION OF THE TARGET AUDIENCE, DRIVE MEANINGFUL ENGAGEMENT, AND CONVERT READERS TO LOYAL CUSTOMERS.

HOW TO WRITE VIRAL LONGFORM THREADS

CREATE VIRAL LONG-FORM THREADS TO ENGAGE AND CONVERT FOR YOUR AUDIENCE

STEP 1. HOOK THE READER WITH A COMPELLING OPENING

PURPOSE: GRAB THEIR ATTENTION IMMEDIATELY.

DETAILS: START WITH A HOOK QUESTION, A BOLD DECLARATION, OR AN INTERESTING FACT.

FOR EXAMPLE, "MOST PEOPLE THINK GOING VIRAL IS LUCK—IT'S NOT. HERE'S THE FORMULA I USED TO GROW MY FOLLOWING BY 200%."

STEP 2: INTRODUCE A RELATABLE STORY

PURPOSE: BUILD TRUST AND HUMAN CONNECTION.

DETAILS: SHARE A PERSONAL OR CLIENT STORY RELEVANT TO YOUR AUDIENCE STRUGGLES.

HIGHLIGHT HOW THE CHALLENGES ALIGN WITH THEIRS, SUCH AS: "A YEAR AGO, I WAS FAILING TO BREAK 1,000 FOLLOWERS. TODAY, I SHARE INSIGHTS WITH AN AUDIENCE OF TENS OF THOUSANDS. HERE'S HOW I DID IT.".

STEP 3. PRACTICAL INSIGHTS AT WORK PURPOSE: PROVIDE VALUE THROUGH EXPERT POSITIONING. OVERVIEW: APPLY PRACTICAL INFORMATION IN CLEAR SUB-SECTIONS.

EXAMPLE:

• "#1: ENGAGE FIRST—CONNECT WITH YOUR AUDIENCE THROUGH AUTHENTIC QUESTIONS."

• "#2: QUALITY OVER QUANTITY—BECOME A MASTER OF ONE THING AT A TIME.

STEP 4. KEEP IT CONVERSATIONAL PURPOSE: TO KEEP THE READERS INTERESTED.

DETAILS: WRITE IN THE SAME WAY YOU WOULD CONVERSE WITH A FRIEND. USE EVERYDAY WORDS, SHORT SENTENCES, AND, OCCASIONALLY, HUMOR AND RHETORICAL QUESTIONS.

STEP 5. APPLY VISUAL BREAKS

PURPOSE: TO MAKE READABILITY.

DETAILS: ADD VISUALS OR USE BOLD AND/OR ITALIC FONT. INSERT SIMPLE DRAWINGS OR APPLY EMOTICONS JUDICIOUSLY TO MAKE IT MORE PERSONABLE.

STEP 6. RAISE THE TENSION AND PROVIDE PROOF

PURPOSE: KEEP THEM ENGAGED.

DETAILS: ANTICIPATE WHAT WILL HAPPEN LATER BY SAYING, "STAY WITH ME-THIS NEXT PART IS KEY" OR "I AM GOING TO GIVE YOU AN EXAMPLE THAT REALLY MAKES THE DIFFERENCE." USE FAST FACTS OR CONSUMER TESTIMONIALS THAT PROVE THE CREDIBILITY.

STEP 7. INSERT A SOFT CTA MID-MESSAGE

PURPOSE: NUDGE WITHOUT FORCING.

DETAILS: BRING YOUR PRODUCT UP LIGHTLY: "IF YOU ENJOY THESE SUGGESTIONS, MY EBOOK, 'TITLE OF THE BOOK,' GOES FURTHER IN MUCH GREATER DETAIL.".

STEP 8. MOTIVATIONAL END WITH A CALL-TO-ACTION

GOAL: ENCOURAGE READERS TO ACT.

OUTLINE: ADD THE MOTIVATION AND SENSE OF URGENCY TO IT BY ENDING WITH: "YOU NOW HAVE THE BLUEPRINT TO LEVELING UP YOUR GAME IN CONTENT. ARE YOU READY? GET 'TITLE OF THE BOOK' AND BEGIN YOUR JOURNEY NOW." ADD THE LINK TO FOLLOW AND REMIND ALL THE BENEFITS.

STEP 9. CALL TO ACTION

PURPOSE: ENGAGEMENT AND VISIBILITY.

EXPLAIN: END WITH A QUESTION SUCH AS, "WHICH OF THESE STRATEGIES WILL YOU TRY FIRST?" CHALLENGE THE READER TO REPLY, SHARE, OR DM YOU FOR MORE INFORMATION.

STEP 10: FOLLOW-UP WITH CONTINUED VALUE

PURPOSE: KEEP THE MOMENTUM GOING.

DETAILS: SHARE FOLLOW-UP RELATED LONGER THREADS THAT TAKE A POINT RAISED AND DIG INTO IT FURTHER. USE COMMENTS OR SHARES TO INFORM YOUR NEW CONTENT, THEREBY CREATING A FEEDBACK LOOP OF INTEREST AND TRUST.

BY WEAVING THESE TOGETHER INTO LONG-FORM THREADS, YOU WILL ENGAGE YOUR AUDIENCE PROFOUNDLY, ENCOURAGE ACTION, AND TURN INTERESTED PARTIES INTO PAYING CUSTOMERS WHO HAVE COME TO TRUST AND VALUE YOUR EXPERTISE.

THE ONLINE WRITING GUIDELINES

HOW TO WRITE ONLINE TO PRODUCE VIRAL THREADS AND CONVERT PEOPLE

1. KNOW YOUR AUDIENCE INSIDE AND OUT

RULE: KNOW THEIR PAIN POINTS, WANTS, AND QUESTIONS. APPLICATION: UNDERSTAND WHO YOUR IDEAL TARGET DEMOGRAPHICS AND PSYCHOGRAPHICS ARE. USE SIMPLE LANGUAGE AND INCLUDE RELEVANT EXAMPLES THAT THEY CAN IDENTIFY WITH.

2. HOOK RULE: GRAB ATTENTION USING THE FIRST SENTENCE. PRACTICE USE STATISTICS THAT ARE SHOCKING; MAKE BOLD STATEMENTS OR QUESTIONS THAT APPEAL.

FOR **EXAMPLE,** "DID YOU KNOW 80% OF VIRAL CONTENT FOLLOWS THESE SIMPLE RULES?"

3. DELIVER VALUE RULE: EACH SECTION TEACHES, INSPIRES OR ENTERTAINS. PRACTICE SHARE ACTIONABLE TIPS, UNIQUE INSIGHTS THAT ARE EASY TO APPLY AND SOLUTIONS.

4. WRITE IN A CONVERSATIONAL TONE RULE: INVOLVE YOUR READERS AS IF YOU WERE SPEAKING TO YOUR BEST FRIEND.

APPLICATION: USE ORDINARY LANGUAGE, CONTRACTIONS, AND THE RIGHT PLACES FOR HUMOR. BE ABLE TO ASK RHETORICAL QUESTIONS AND PERSONAL STORIES.

5. STORYTELLING FOR CREDIBILITY RULE: IT'S TRUE THAT PEOPLE CONNECT BEST TO STORIES.

APPLICATION: USE MINI-STORIES OR CASE STUDIES THAT EXPLAIN COMMON PROBLEMS AND SOLUTIONS.

6. BREAK UP LONG TEXT WITH FORMATTING RULE: MAKE CONTENT SCANNABLE.

APPLICATION: USE SUBHEADINGS, BULLET POINTS, SHORT PARAGRAPHS, BOLD KEY INSIGHTS, AND EMOJIS.

7. BUILD ANTICIPATION AND INCLUDE THE PROOF RULE: TEASE THE NEXT POINT AND BUILD CREDIBILITY.

APPLICATION: USE PHRASES LIKE "THIS NEXT TIP TRANSFORMED MY ENGAGEMENT" AND BACK IT UP WITH SCREENSHOTS, DATA, OR TESTIMONIALS.

8. SOFTER MID-THREAD CTA RULE: BRING UP YOUR OFFER WITHOUT TRYING TOO HARD TO CLOSE THE DEAL.

USE APPLICATION: INCLUDE A SOFT CTA SUCH AS THIS: "LOVE THESE INSIGHTS? IT GOES TO A WHOLE OTHER LEVEL IN MY EBOOK, 'THREADS TO MILLIONS'."

9. END WITH A STRONG CTA RULE: END WITH A STRONG, CONCRETE CALL-TO ACTION.

USE APPLICATION: A CLOSING LINE LIKE THIS, "LEVEL UP YOUR CONTENT? GRAB 'TITLE OF THE BOOK' TODAY!" AND THEN INCLUDE A LINK FOLLOWED BY REMINDING THEM OF THE BENEFITS.

10. ENGAGE THE AUDIENCE RULE: CONCLUDE BY ASKING A QUESTION OR CHALLENGING READERS TO CONTRIBUTE THEIR PERSONAL EXPERIENCE: "WHAT IS YOUR SECRET WEAPON TO KEEPING AUDIENCES HOOKED?"

11. BE CONSISTENT RULE: CONSISTENTLY DEPICT YOUR BRAND VOICE AND FREQUENCY.

APPLICATION: REINFORCE FAMILIARITY AND BUILD UP TRUST BY POSTING REGULARLY THROUGH THE CREATION OF VALUABLE, RELEVANT CONTENT.

12. FOLLOW-UP ADDITIONAL VALUE RULE: END CONTINUE THE CONVERSATION.

APPLICATION: POST FOLLOW-UP THREADS OR JOIN COMMENTS TO DEEPEN RELATIONSHIPS AND KEEP YOUR AUDIENCE INVESTED .

THESE RULES IN APPLICATION SHALL HELP YOU CREATE ENGAGEMENT THREADS THAT INSPIRE ACTION AND CONVERT YOUR READERS TO LOYAL, PAYING CUSTOMERS.

ADVANCED TIPS FOR VIRAL THREADS THAT CONVERT

1. EXPERTISE APPLICATION OF THE RULE OF SEQUENCING:

MAKE YOUR THREAD CURIOSITY-DRIVEN/BUILD CURIOSITY: HELP YOUR READER FEEL CURIOUS AS YOU CREATE A SEQUENTIAL STRUCTURE FOR YOUR THREAD.

APPLICATION: USE A PROGRESSION THAT TEASES THE NEXT POINT. DANGLE A BAITING STATEMENT AS AN OPENER, THEN GO INTO IMPACTFUL INSIGHTS, AND END WITH A POWERFUL CONCLUSION. HAVE EVERY ONE OF YOUR TWEETS FALL ORGANICALLY ONTO THE NEXT ONE.

2. MAKE USE OF DATA AND SOCIAL PROOF

RULE: MAKE USE OF PROVEN FACTS FOR AUTHENTICITY. USE CASE STUDIES, STATISTICS, OR EVEN YOUR OWN EXPERIENCE TO FURTHER BUILD UP TRUST.

EXAMPLE: "I PUT THIS INTO ACTION AND GAINED 200% MORE ENGAGEMENT"— SUPPORTED BY A SCREENSHOT OR TESTIMONIAL.

3. CONTENT RULE: MAKE IT SHAREABLE AND RELATABLE.

APPLICATION: DRAW FROM THE EMOTIONAL OR THE BATTLEGROUND SHARED IN EVERYDAY EXPERIENCES. A "YOU'RE NOT ALONE" MOMENT. PEOPLE WILL SHARE IF THEY SEE THEMSELVES IN YOUR STORY.

4. RULE OF USING CONTRASTING

EXAMPLES: PROVIDE THE 'BEFORE AND AFTER' EXPERIENCE.

IMPLEMENTATION: HIGHLIGHT EXAMPLES BOTH WITH AND WITHOUT YOUR APPROACH. THAT GRAPHIC CONTRAST WILL IMBED VALUE THAT SUPPORTS THE USEFULNESS OF YOUR TECHNIQUE, COMPELLING READERS TO DO SOMETHING.

5. RULE OF USING GRAPHICS: USE IMAGES OR ICONS TO MAKE AN IMPRESSION.

IMPLEMENTATION: THREADS ARE MORE NOTICEABLE IN FEEDS THAT INCLUDE IMAGES. UTILIZE INFOGRAPHICS, HEADLINES, OR MEME-BASED GRAPHICS RELATED TO YOUR MESSAGE TO CALL ATTENTION TO KEY POINTS.

6. STARTING WITH OPEN-ENDED QUESTIONS RULE:

ENGAGE TO INCREASE THE REACH OF THE THREAD APPLICATION: END OFF TWEETS WITH QUESTIONS LIKE "WHAT DO YOU THINK ABOUT THIS?" OR "HAVE YOU EVER USED THIS METHOD?" THIS ACTUALLY WILL ENCOURAGE COMMENTS AND RESPONSES FROM OTHER PEOPLE.

7. PRINCIPLE: PROVIDE PERSONAL INSIGHT AND TAKEAWAYS

ESTABLISH AUTHORITY: SHARE UNUSUAL THINGS YOU HAVE LEARNED FROM YOUR ANALYSIS.

APPLICATION: USE PHRASES SUCH AS, "HERE IS WHAT I LEARNED AFTER ANALYZING 1,000 VIRAL THREADS," THEN PROVIDE CRISP INSIGHTS. READERS LIKE TO KNOW INFORMATION THEY WON'T FIND ANYWHERE ELSE.

8. PLACE SUBTLE CTAS THROUGHOUT
RULE: DON'T WAIT UNTIL THE END TO ENGAGE YOUR AUDIENCE.

APPLICATION: STRATEGICALLY PLACE CTAS WITHIN THE BODY, SUCH AS "IF THIS RESONATES, CHECK OUT MY EBOOK FOR MORE." THIS KEEPS READERS AWARE OF YOUR OFFER AS THEY ENGAGE.

9. RULE OF URGENCY ANGLE: INDUCE FOMO. APPLICATION: USE WORDS LIKE "ONLY FOR A LIMITED TIME AVAILABLE" OR "EARLY ADOPTERS WILL BENEFIT MOST FROM THESE STRATEGIES." THIS ESTABLISHES URGENCY.

10. RULE TO AMPLIFY REACH WITH COLLABORATIONS: TEAM UP WITH CREATORS THAT COMPLEMENT YOUR NICHE. APPLICATION: CO-AUTHOR THREADS OR CROSS-PROMOTE WITH OTHER INFLUENCERS IN YOUR NICHE. IT TAPS INTO THEIR AUDIENCE, MAKING YOU MORE SEEN AND GENERALLY CREDIBLE.

11. CONTINUOUSLY ANALYZE AND OPTIMIZE, THE RULE OF USING DATA TO REFINE YOUR APPROACH

APPLY THIS RULE THROUGH REVIEWING THREAD PERFORMANCE METRICS, INCLUDING LIKES, SHARES, AND COMMENTS, IDENTIFY WHICH TACTICS RESONATE MOST. DOUBLE DOWN ON THOSE PIECES.

12. END WITH IMPACTFUL CTAS RULE:
ENSURE THAT THE FINAL TWEET IS MEMORABLE AND ALSO ACTION-ORIENTED.

APPLICATION: USE PHRASES SUCH AS, "WANT TO TAKE YOUR SKILLS UP A NOTCH? DM ME FOR EXCLUSIVE TIPS" OR "ARE YOU READY TO GET STARTED? GET 'TITLE OF THE BOOK' NOW."

BY USING THESE ADVANCED TACTICS, YOU ARE PRETTY MUCH ON YOUR WAY TO CREATING THREADS THAT WILL ENGAGE AND CHAT UP YOUR AUDIENCE AND CONVERT THEM FROM READERS INTO LOYAL CUSTOMERS.

BONUS

50+ VIRAL HOOK TEMPLATES FOR INSTAGRAM THREADS WITH EXAMPLES

ENGAGING INSTAGRAM THREADS WITH EXAMPLES:

YOU CAN BEGIN USING IT FOR ANY NICHE YOU WANT YOUR AUDIENCE TO GET ENGAGED IN AND CONVERT INTO SALES.

1."DO YOU KNOW YOU'RE DOING THIS?"

EXAMPLE: DO YOU KNOW YOU'RE DOING THIS IN YOUR SKINCARE ROUTINE?

2."HERE'S WHY [COMMON BELIEF] IS WRONG."

EXAMPLE: HERE'S WHY DRINKING 8 GLASSES OF WATER A DAY MIGHT NOT BE ENOUGH.

3. "YOU DON'T NEED [X] TO GET [Y]."

EXAMPLE: YOU DON'T NEED FANCY GEAR TO GET FIT. HERE'S WHAT REALLY MATTERS.

4. "THE SECRET TO [THE DESIRED OUTCOME] NOBODY TALKS ABOUT."

EXAMPLE: THE SECRET TO GLOWING SKIN THAT NOBODY TALKS ABOUT.

5. "I WAS TODAY YEARS OLD WHEN I LEARNED [SURPRISING FACT]."

EXAMPLE: I WAS TODAY YEARS OLD WHEN I LEARNED THAT GREEN TEA CAN BOOST METABOLISM NATURALLY.

6. "[NUMBER] THINGS I WISH I KNEW BEFORE [ACTIVITY OR EVENT]."

EXAMPLE: 5 THINGS I WISH I KNEW BEFORE SWITCHING TO AN ALL-NATURAL DIET.

7. "WHY [SPECIFIC OUTCOME] CHANGED EVERYTHING FOR ME."

EXAMPLE: WHY STARTING MY DAY WITH MEDITATION CHANGED EVERYTHING FOR ME.

8. "I DID [SPECIFIC THING] FOR [X] DAYS. HERE'S WHAT HAPPENED."

EXAMPLE: I TRIED AYURVEDIC HERBS FOR 30 DAYS. HERE'S WHAT HAPPENED.

9. "[X] REASONS WHY [ACTIVITY OR METHOD] DOESN'T WORK (AND WHAT DOES)."

EXAMPLE: 3 REASONS WHY DIETING DOESN'T WORK (AND WHAT ACTUALLY DOES).

10. "WHAT NO ONE TELLS YOU ABOUT [TOPIC]."

EXAMPLE: WHAT NO ONE TELLS YOU ABOUT INTERMITTENT FASTING.

11. "THIS [ITEM] CHANGED MY LIFE."

EXAMPLE: THIS SIMPLE MORNING RITUAL CHANGED MY LIFE.

12. "STOP DOING THIS IF YOU WANT [DESIRED RESULT]."

EXAMPLE: STOP DOING THIS IF YOU WANT CLEARER SKIN.".

13. "IF I ONLY GAVE ONE TIP ABOUT [TOPIC], THIS WOULD BE IT."

EXAMPLE: IF ONLY ONE TIP EXISTED ABOUT BALANCING HORMONES, THIS WOULD BE IT.

14. "THE MOST UNDERRATED [METHOD/PRODUCT] FOR [RESULT]."

EXAMPLE: THE MOST UNDERRATED SPICE FOR DIGESTION.

15. "I DIDN'T BELIEVE IT UNTIL I TRIED IT."

EXAMPLE: I DIDN'T BELIEVE IN OIL PULLING UNTIL I TRIED IT.

16. "WHAT [FAMOUS PERSON] GETS WRONG ABOUT [TOPIC]?"

EXAMPLE: WHAT MOST CELEBRITIES GET WRONG ABOUT DIETING.

17. "THAT'S ALL ABOUT [TOPIC] IN ONE THREAD."

EXAMPLE: THAT'S ALL ABOUT MANAGING STRESS NATURALLY IN ONE THREAD.

18. "IF YOU HAVE [PROBLEM], TRY THIS."

EXAMPLE: IF YOU HAVE LOW ENERGY, TRY THIS.

19. "WHY [COMMON ADVICE] IS WRONG AND WHAT TO DO INSTEAD."

EXAMPLE: WHY 'EATING LESS' DOESN'T WORK FOR LONG-TERM WEIGHT LOSS.

20. "I DID [UNIQUE METHOD] FOR [X] DAYS. HERE'S MY HONEST REVIEW."

EXAMPLE: I DID AN AYURVEDIC DETOX FOR 7 DAYS. HERE'S MY HONEST REVIEW.

21. "DO THIS IF YOU WANT [DESIRED OUTCOME]."

EXAMPLE: DO THIS IF YOU WANT BETTER SLEEP.

22. "DON'T START [ACTIVITY] UNTIL YOU READ THIS."

EXAMPLE: DON'T START A NEW SUPPLEMENT UNTIL YOU READ THIS.

23. "THE REAL REASON WHY [THE PROBLEM] IS SO COMMON."

EXAMPLE: WHAT'S REALLY GOING ON WITH STRESS (AND WHAT TO DO ABOUT IT)?

24. "HOW I TRANSITIONED FROM [STARTING POINT] TO [SUCCESS POINT]."

EXAMPLE: HOW I WENT FROM BEING PERPETUALLY EXHAUSTED TO HAVING ENERGY ALL DAY.

25. "WHAT NOBODY IS TELLING YOU ABOUT [TOPIC] FROM [INFLUENCER/EXPERT]."

EXAMPLE: WHAT MOST EXPERTS AREN'T TELLING YOU ABOUT CLEAN EATING.

26. "THE BIGGEST LIE ABOUT [TOPIC]— DECONSTRUCTED."

EXAMPLE: THE BIGGEST LIE ABOUT ANTI-AGING SKINCARE—DEBUNKED.

27. "THIS IS WHAT [X] REALLY LOOKS LIKE."

EXAMPLE: THIS IS WHAT DETOXING ACTUALLY LOOKS LIKE (AND IT'S NOT JUST JUICE CLEANSES).

28. "THINK YOU KNOW EVERYTHING ABOUT [TOPIC]? THINK AGAIN."

EXAMPLE: THINK YOU KNOW EVERYTHING ABOUT HOW TO IMPROVE IMMUNITY? THINK AGAIN.

29. "THE [NUMBER] BEST WAYS TO [ACHIEVE GOAL] WITHOUT [SACRIFICE."

EXAMPLE: THE 7 BEST WAYS TO BOOST ENERGY WITHOUT CAFFEINE.

30. "HOW [SMALL CHANGE] CAN MAKE A BIG DIFFERENCE IN [AREA OF LIFE].".

EXAMPLE: HOW A 5-MINUTE MORNING ROUTINE CAN CHANGE EVERYTHING IN YOUR MOOD.

31. "WHAT I WISH I KNEW ABOUT [TOPIC] BEFORE [X]."

EXAMPLE: WHAT I WISH I KNEW ABOUT PROBIOTICS BEFORE BUYING THEM.

32. "[TOPIC] MADE SIMPLE: YOUR ULTIMATE GUIDE."

EXAMPLE: AYURVEDA MADE SIMPLE: YOUR ULTIMATE GUIDE TO STARTING OUT.

33. "I MADE [COMMON MISTAKE],A COMMON AND HERE'S WHAT I LEARNED."

EXAMPLE: I MADE THE MISTAKE OF OVEREXERCISING. HERE'S WHAT I LEARNED.

34. "X UNEXPECTED BENEFITS OF [MOST UNEXPECTED TOPIC]."

EXAMPLE: 5 UNEXPECTED BENEFITS OF USING TURMERIC IN YOUR SKINCARE ROUTINE

35. "THIS IS WHAT [X] DOESN'T TEACH YOU ABOUT [Y]."

EXAMPLE: THIS IS WHAT MEDICAL SCHOOL DOESN'T TEACH YOU ABOUT HOLISTIC WELLNESS

36. "WHAT I LEARNED AFTER [ACTIVITY OR EVENT]."

EXAMPLE: WHAT I LEARNED AFTER TRYING HERBAL REMEDIES FOR A MONTH

37. "THE TRUTH ABOUT [TRENDING TOPIC]."

EXAMPLE: THE TRUTH ABOUT ADAPTOGENS AND WHY EVERYONE'S TALKING ABOUT THEM.

38. "IF YOU'RE SICK OF [PROBLEM], TRY THIS."

EXAMPLE: IF YOU'RE SICK OF BEING BLOATED, TRY THIS EASY FIX.

39. "EVER WONDERED WHY [SITUATION] HAPPENS? HERE'S THE ANSWER."

EXAMPLE: EVER WONDERED WHY YOU GET SLEEPY AFTER LUNCH? HERE'S THE ANSWER.

40. "THE [ADJECTIVE] SIDE OF [TOPIC]."

EXAMPLE: THE HIDDEN SIDE OF ESSENTIAL OILS.

41. "[TOPIC] IS TRENDING, BUT IS IT WORTH THE HYPE?"

EXAMPLE: COLLAGEN SUPPLEMENTS ARE ALL THE RAGE, BUT ARE THEY WORTH THE FUSS?

42. "HOW TO [DESIRABLE ACTION] WITHOUT [UNDESIRED OUTCOME]."

EXAMPLE: HOW TO LOSE WEIGHT WITHOUT COUNTING CALORIES.

43. "WHAT'S THE DEAL WITH [HOT TOPIC]?"

EXAMPLE: WHAT'S THE DEAL WITH MATCHA LATTES?

44. "I QUIT [BAD HABIT], AND HERE IS WHAT CHANGED."

EXAMPLE: I QUIT SUGAR, AND HERE'S WHAT CHANGED.

45. "DON'T LET [COMMON OBSTACLE] GET IN THE WAY."

EXAMPLE: DON'T LET BRAIN FOG HOLD YOU BACK. HERE'S HOW TO BEAT IT.

46. "WHEN I BEGAN DOING [NEW HABIT], EVERYTHING SHIFTED."

EXAMPLE: EVERYTHING ABOUT MY STRESS LEVELS CHANGED WHEN I STARTED JOURNALING.

47. "THE [NUMBER] EASIEST STEPS TO [DESIRED RESULT]."

EXAMPLE: THE 3 EASIEST STEPS TO IMPROVE YOUR DIGESTION.

48. "THE ONE THING YOU NEED TO KNOW ABOUT [TOPIC]."

EXAMPLE: THE ONE THING YOU NEED TO KNOW ABOUT DETOXIFYING YOUR LIVER.

49. "WANT [RESULT]? STOP DOING THIS."

EXAMPLE: WANT CLEARER SKIN? STOP OVER-EXFOLIATING.

50. "I'VE TRIED THEM ALL. HERE'S WHAT ACTUALLY WORKS FOR [PROBLEM].".

EXAMPLE: I'VE TRIED ALL THE HERBAL TEAS. HERE'S WHAT ACTUALLY WORKS FOR CALMING ANXIETY.

51. "IF YOU THINK [MISCONCEPTION], YOU NEED TO READ THIS."

EXAMPLE: IF YOU THINK ALL FATS ARE BAD, YOU NEED TO READ THIS.

52. "WHY I SWITCHED FROM [COMMON METHOD] TO [NEW METHOD]."

EXAMPLE: WHY I SWITCHED FROM REGULAR SKINCARE PRODUCTS TO AN ALL-NATURAL ROUTINE.

53. "[X] FACTS YOU NEED TO KNOW ABOUT [TOPIC]."

EXAMPLE: 10 THINGS YOU WANT TO KNOW ABOUT USING AYURVEDA IN YOUR LIFE.

54. "HOW TO [ACHIEVE GOAL] WITHOUT EXPERIENCING [COMMON FRUSTRATION]."

EXAMPLE: HOW TO SLEEP BETTER WITHOUT WAKING UP GROGGY.

55. "LET'S TALK ABOUT [TABOO OR MISUNDERSTOOD TOPIC]."

EXAMPLE: LET'S TALK ABOUT HORMONE BALANCE AND WHY IT MATTERS.

56. I LEARNED THIS THE HARD WAY, SO YOU DON'T HAVE TO."

EXAMPLE: I QUICKLY LEARNED THE HARD LESSON THAT NOT ALL SUPPLEMENTS ARE CREATED EQUAL.

57."A BEGINNER'S GUIDE TO [TOPIC]."

EXAMPLE: A BEGINNER'S GUIDE TO HERBAL TINCTURES AND THEIR USES.

THANK YOU

VISIT US: WWW.DOKETS.SHOP

www.ingramcontent.com/pod-product-compliance
Lightning Source LLC
Chambersburg PA
CBHW030043230526
45472CB00005B/1645

* 9 7 9 8 3 0 0 2 0 0 3 3 6 *